A Play For Puppets
A Play in Three Acts

By

Hi Ka Lu

Drawings by the Author

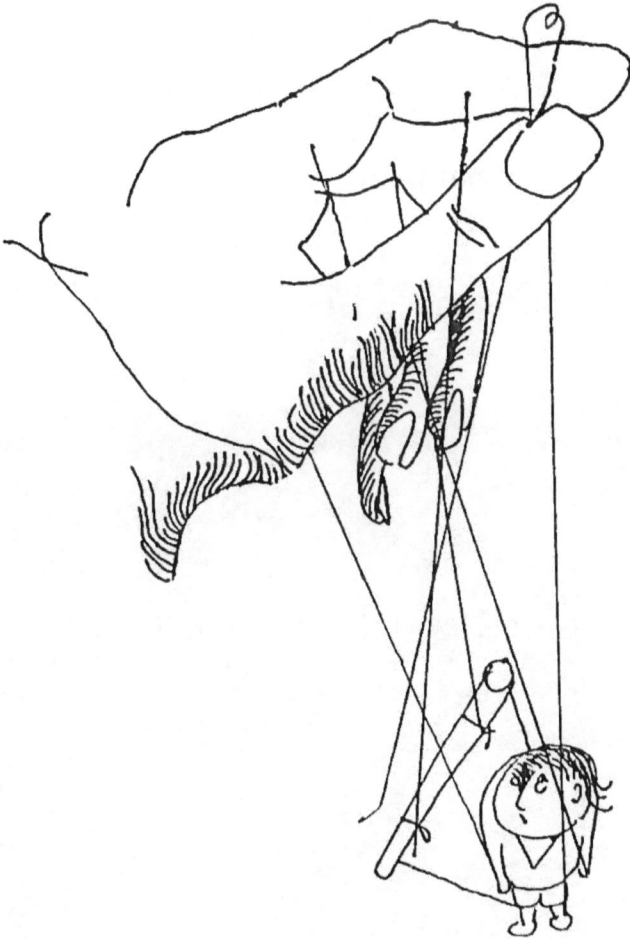

Copyright 1986 by Hi Ka Lu
All Rights Reserved By The Author
Printed by Sanctuary Press, The Classic Letterpress
Santa Fe, New Mexico, USA
ISBN: 978-1-7378076-0-5 assigned Aug 2021,
Dave Mysite Dot Com All Rights Reserved

To Sarai

ACT I

There are actors. Let them be marked: First Female, One Actor, Somebody, The Leader, etc. The scene is here... the mountains, the shore, the streets of the town... and the people. There's always at least one on stage...

ONE ACTOR: Why do you sit down so soon? You don't see me doing it - - - too soon. You don't know where you're going and you don't know how to get there. So you sit down too soon, a drop out of the kitchen faucet... plop-sit...plop-sit...plopsit.. next day...plop --------------------sit, every day another...plopsit... plopsit...plop...sit, every day another ...plop-sit...plopsit...plop...sit, you don't see me doing that ...I Dooooo! I have my work cut out for me (*turns to audience, fiercely*) I'm talking to <u>you</u>. <u>I'm</u> talking, please! Hell, I'm not actoring; I'm talking... play! It's true, somebody is putting the words in my mouth... but I can change that any time.... Watch (*ad lib from here as long as you like but tell them so they will know it; continue to prove it to them*)...so you see, I'm not something hanging on a string. I say what I want! I'm not afraid O.K. maybe I'll have a son or a daughter who's less afraid, who can say it for me...you'll see.
ANOTHER ACTOR: Where milk and honey flows...I'm just asking...why does the road have to be like that?...the blood.. all that pain.. and all that decay...I really have to see the dentist... damn... I just don't have the money.... and my mouth is rotting out...
ONE ACTOR: You're a fool... you just don't ask stupid questions like that... see the dentist... and work!...so you can pay the dentist!
THIRD ACTOR: I'm not afraid to die.. but I swear to you, before I go I'm taking one of those bastards with me...the blood suckers.

ANOTHER ACTOR: Where milk and honey flows.. they got killer-prisons.. you can put them away in there… put them in there, get'em killed… and you don't see them anymore.. you stay pure.. no blame.. if you're still in trouble, maybe you go see the great man.. hell, out there in the audience maybe.. one of you knows? Where milk and honey flows, there's no audience left.. only stones.. for witnesses.. <u>Right</u>? Were any of you ever.. yeah, that's not possible, if you'd been there you couldn't stand sitting here.. watching.. for entertainment.. I bet you don't like me so much.. well I don't like you either… You think I could like you? (*long pause*). You didn't need to answer. There's no audience!

ONE ACTOR: You stupid bastard.. there's always an audience left… 'till the very end.

THIRD ACTOR: He was never there himself.. talks about where milk and honey flows.. all he knows is his own anger.. at others he envies for being safe… who's safe?...ever… I'm not afraid (*ad lib, does not have to be verbal, movement is probably freer.*)

ANOTHER ACTOR: (*breaks in boldly, these are his own revelations*) Look, I go to the sea or the mountains and I sit. I meditate, you know… can't stand television all the time…I'd just as soon get rid of the set, but the family wants it… it's the only place left where milk and honey flows… with every commercial. I've really nothing against chewing gum and candy…it's so bad for your teeth, I don't eat it much (*Third Actor offers him a candy-bar…he accepts perfunctorily without thanking*). I just can't get it together (*chews with gusto*) how do I work and dance at the same time… I don't like it when they criticize… they're all blind….if they weren't so blind I could get it together…I could make good money… and the job discriminations, they were just talking about it on TV last night…how can I get it together like that? Doesn't even leave me enough to go to the movies… hell, at least I'm free (*this is said with abandon but without conviction*).

(*They're bringing in a mountain constructed of paper*)

ONE ACTOR: (*has been helping to bring in the mountian…now he steps forward, slightly out of breath…all the others go their own way*) I made that you know…I did it!

ANOTHER ACTOR: (*looking around at the others*) They were never together. Not the English, not the Americans, not the Indians, not the Chinese, not the Germans, not the Russians…

(*All other actors now begin chiming in*): Not the Litvaks, not the Gambians, not the Japs, not the Anglos, not the Kikes, not the Coons, not the Kooks, not the Pauls, not the Mathews, not the Lukes… (*all in unison*) not the etcetera, etcetera, etcetera, etcetera, etcetera, etcetera…

THIRD ACTOR: Oh Stop!

(*All continue wordlessly, a kind of chaotic dance now. A leader is bound to emerge here, it's the way things are, and then things are a little more synchronized*).

THE LEADER: (*as predicted....and he can be recognized because he stops dancing and utters this sound*) Aaaaaaaaaaaaaaaah! (*he's projecting energy into the audience. This sound emerges from a high inner concentration...the mouth is fully open, as it rises from an area just below the navel, the neurological center..*) Aaaaaaaaaaaaaaaah!

THIRD ACTOR: (*steps forward moving toward audience...if audience is seated, he moves directly into the audience*) Say Aaaaaaaaaaaaaaah! He's the doctor. Say Aaaaah! No! Don't laugh.. don't be afraid… there are no tongue-depressors! Say Aaaah! (*urges gently to make audience relax into the sound*) Say it again! Aaaah! This sound is you--- this sound is myself. It's bigger than anything you have been taught in school or church. But even that sound is not God! Say Aaaah! And listen to what is coming out of yourself and let me listen to what is out of me. We are one in that sound! Don't be afraid. This sound is bigger than any *god* they have ever taught us anywhere! But that sound alone is not God!

LEADER: Do you understand then? If you do, say "Oh!" If you aren't sure say, "Oh?" That doesn't commit you to anything, but that's the sound! Say, "Oh"…if…oh…if they ask you, tell them, "That is where my intelligence comes from… all of it" 'How could you know?' they'll ask. Tell them, 'I told you!' (*if there is a reaction in the audience, no matter from where, don't speak--- dance!*)

ANOTHER ACTOR: They need proof out there! (*points to audience, picks out individuals one at a time*) They need to be sure! (*he faces the leader*)

LEADER: The proof is in U (sound 'uuuh')…in the word! Sure…Sure…say, "proof" …say, "U" (sound 'uuuh')…now you know…now you know? Say it a thousand times and you'll begin to be sure…(long pause)…you can't believe this? You can believe it? You don't need to believe it…you're here! Your feet, your hands are touching…your ears are hearing…your eyes…your nose…your tongue tastes. And all say U (*uuuuuuh, that's a sigh*).

ONE ACTOR: (*turns to the leader*) O.K. – O.K., so you're here, so we're all here! I've asked myself, like most everybody has…what for? Why is this the place where I came out and what for? I've heard them say we're all one, but that place where we're all one … that must be so far away. When I came out of my mother's belly, I separated into two…and I've been separated ever since. And all I'm sure about is that I came out here to be buried, everything else is conjecture and as long as that's all I can be sure about, I'm scared and neither Moses, Buddha, nor Christ are much of a tranquilizer… they were all buried…at least once. I'd rather dooo something… when you work you don't have time to think too much…bad thoughts…I had an aunt…she was always afraid of the nights… the nights when the bad thoughts would come. She's buried!

LEADER: Feel your body first (*begins his dance again, the others slowly follow, hesitate, follow with greater confidence.. he stops*). Don't mistake this…we're not here for an orgy…we're here to judge without passing judgement…..That's the hardest exercise you're likely to come across.

(*Props are brought in at various times from now on by various actors… left sitting around, then eventually removed…..without explanations. These objects can be animate or inanimate.*)

ANOTHER ACTOR: Hell man, I'm beginning to think this doesn't help any…it's like singing mantras to get into a higher space…I've sung them and been in Heaven in the morning - - and in Hell-world by afternoon.

THIRD ACTOR: Yes, that's our fear!

ANOTHER ACTOR: (*this song can be repeated more than once, melody, there's no need for that to repeat, eventually an instrument will accompany the song*)

There is a giant hole
Deep down deep in New Mexico
And inside sleeps a dragon
Way down deep in New Mexico
One day he'll leave his cavern
And crawl outside and roar
Then the earth will tremble
And the mountains, they will fall.
Oh dear, Oh what will happen to us all!
He's 4000 years long
That dragon is so very strong
Who'll look the dragon in the eye?

And turn him into a dragon-fly.

Oh, I'd much prefer to watch a dragon-fly…

Aaaah, I'd much prefer to watch a dragon fly.

> (*What occurs now is not permitted to be too clear. Here and there the actors take up the song or snatches of it and invent their own melody. They move into the audience but make no contact in any other way. The audience has ceased to exist for them. The audience may become uneasy if this is done right. If the actors are conscious of themselves in their "right roles" at this moment, the power of this moment will never materialize. The audience now is an experienced phenomenon we don't need to react to. That is the desired sense of the moment.*)

A NEW ONE: The chance of your life! Classes start at 9 a.m. Five years with the great Grand-manser, founder of the block-jump…my own findings…at a price you can afford. Come and block-jump the Omega rhythms. Tomorrow the price may go up. Guarantee….. You come once, you'll come again…

ANOTHER ACTOR: "Never more"

(*All gather around the New One. He's slung on somebody's shoulders… or She's slung…. So far the sexes are irrelevant. The New One is carried off. The audience is not quite sure whether in triumph or disgrace.*)

FIRST FEMALE: In this production I'm marked the first female… I say any female is bound to be first I can tell you.. any woman in labor pains… tell her about Adam's Rib. The mother in our society…

ANOTHER FEMALE: (*she appears from in back of the audience, carrying a few supermarket containers*) Excuse me, I'm from the Co-op… is anybody here interested in fertilized eggs? I'm not sure they're organic, but as you know there is less cholesterol when they are fertilized. I'm sorry to be disturbing, but we'll be closed for two weeks… contact me after the show. I'll be in the rear.

FIRST FEMALE: The importance of motherhood is not the same as the importance of womanhood…. Fertilized eggs… damn this play… what a put down! (*starts free dance*)

THE AUTHOR: (*any creatively occupied individual will do. He's totally preoccupied with himself, mumbles, but loud enough that he can be easily heard*) How do I get to the point? No! That's not it! (*he approaches the audience and persuades a member of the audience to replace him… teaches him to say the lines "How do I get to the point?"*)

SECOND FEMALE: In this production I'm the second female. I'm marked and that's my job.. to clear the decks! Everybody….. prepare for battle stations! From here on I give the orders. I'M captain of the starship *Enterprise*? If there ever was another one he's been hiding. Mister. Alright, lets go take your places… No phasers! No Lasers! No force shields! This is the real thing. Don't let those yellow-bellied bastards out there sit it out (*she makes it apparent that she means the audience and an actor planted among the audience cuts in, "That's the wrong way!"*) that's exactly the way…. That keeps us out of battles (*laughs derisively*), but… Northern Lights! (*she says this like a curse*)…. It doesn't keep us from suffering! (*laughs*)

LEADER: (*re-appears*) O.K. O.K. We must do this the right way, otherwise it's all for nothing.

ANOTHER ACTOR: He should be paid for doing this for us. He resolutely must be paid!

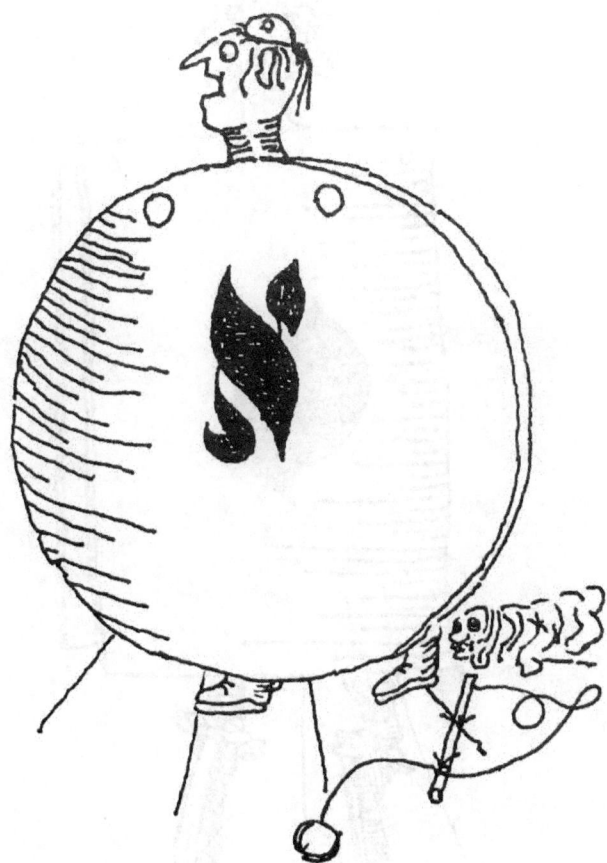

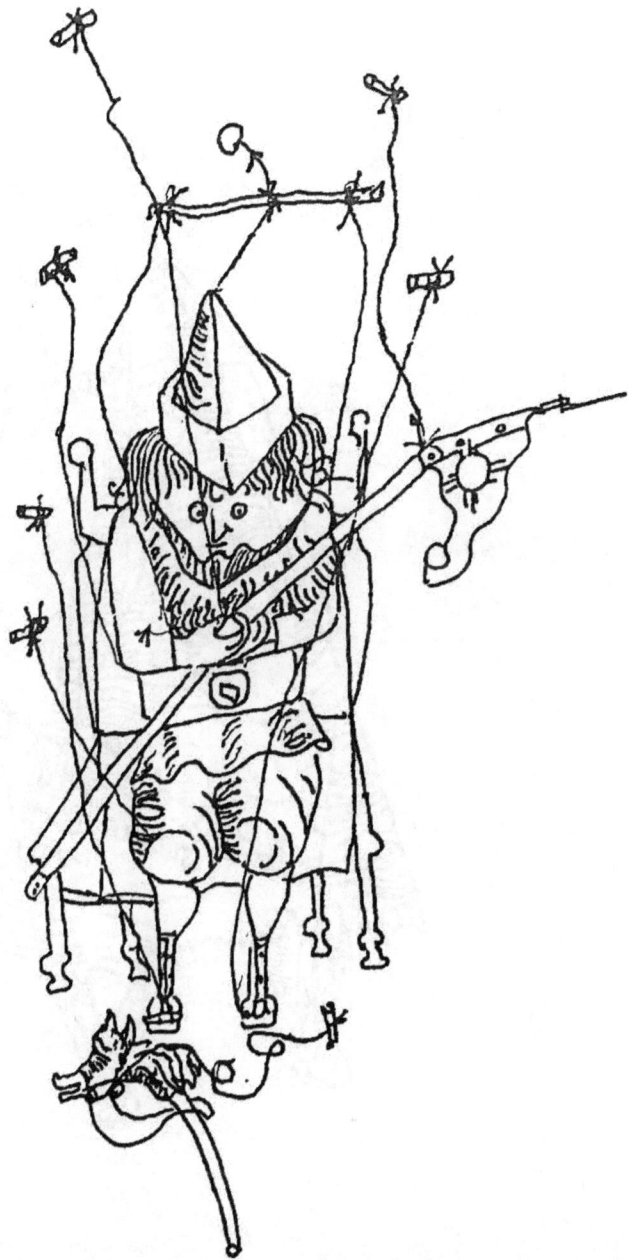

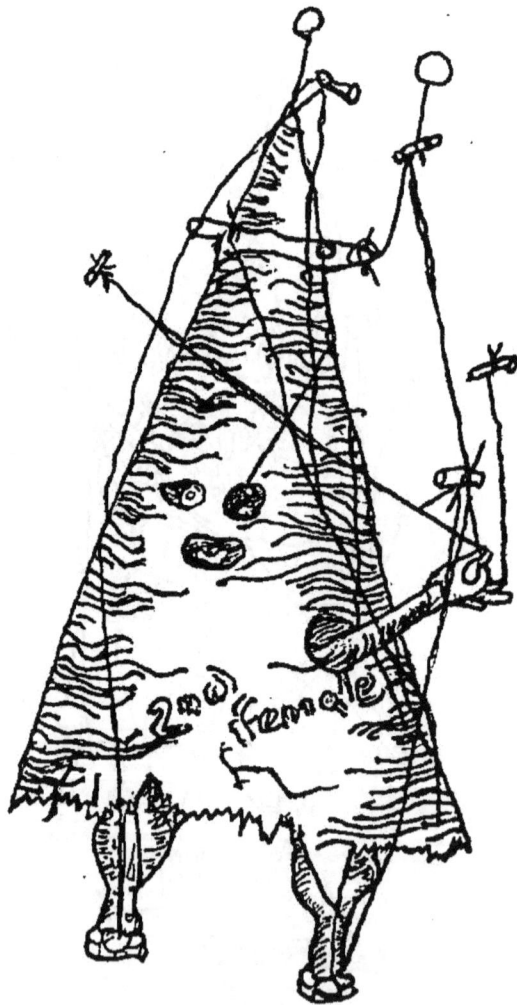

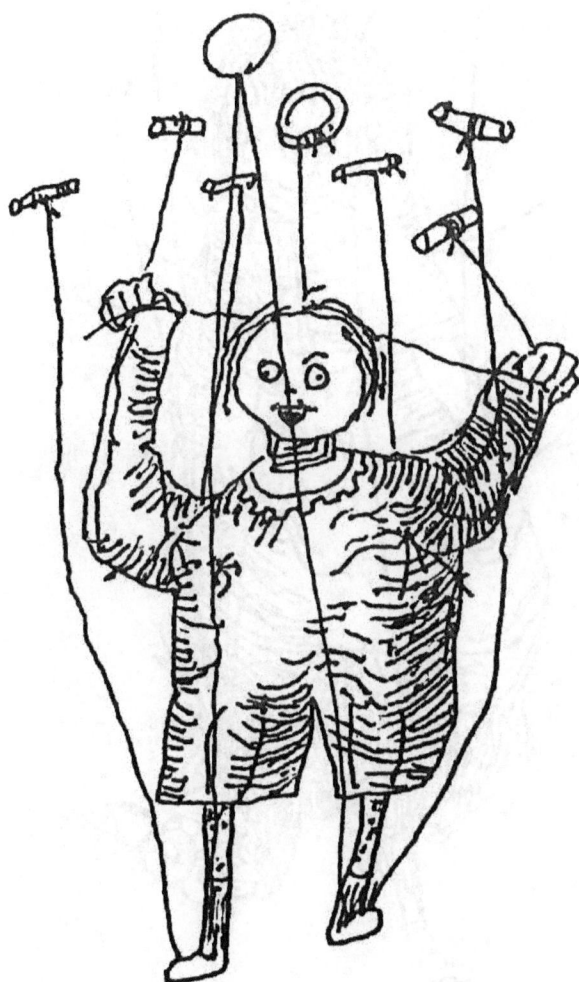

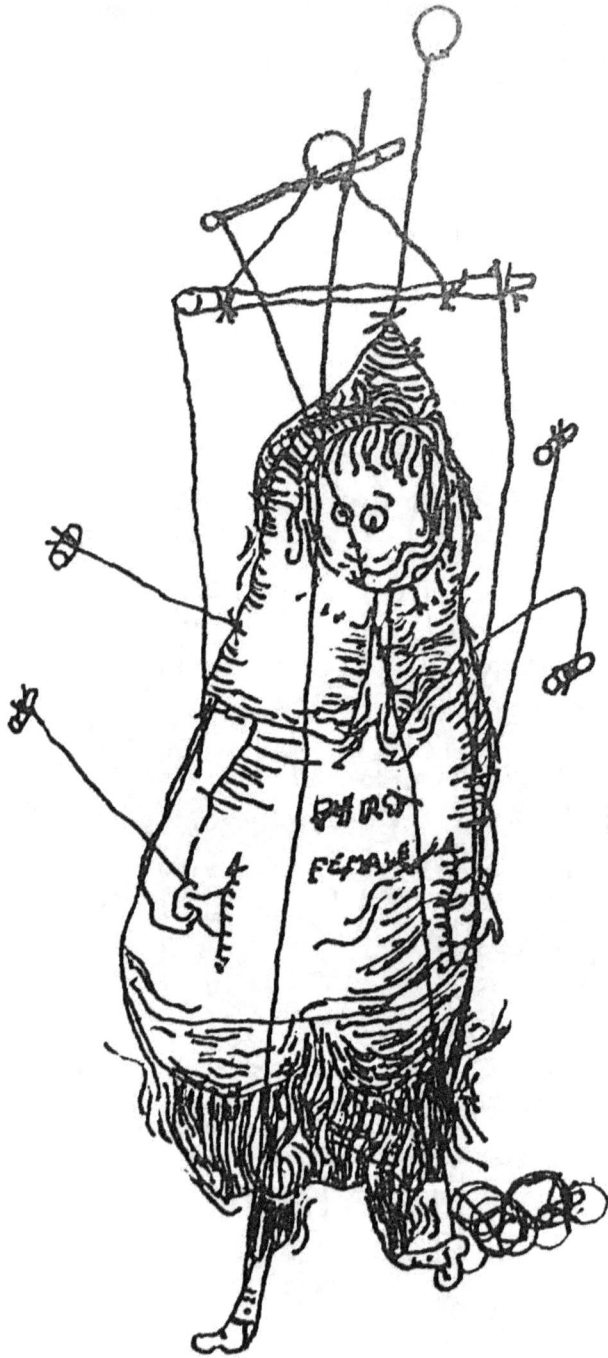

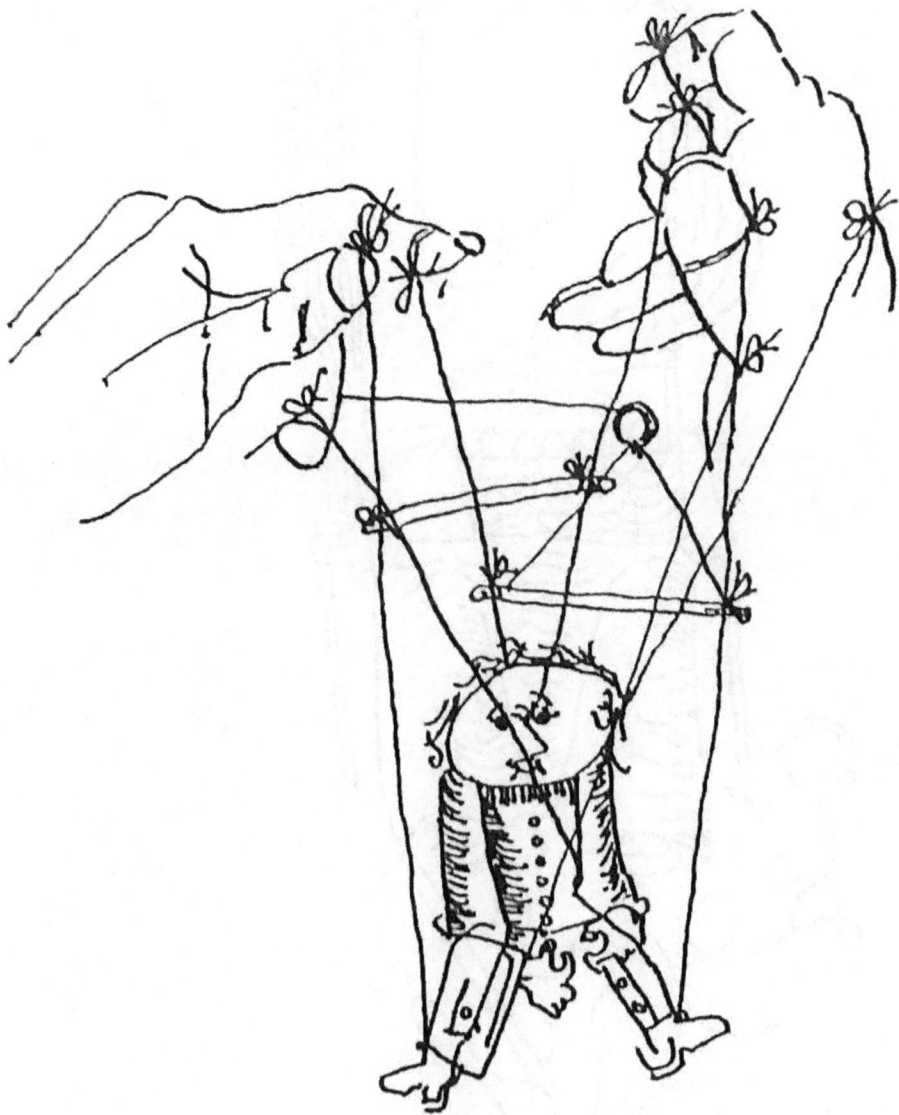

ONE ACTOR: The leader must be paid.. absolutely!

FIRST FEMALE: You guys better see if there'll be any money left to pay him with, after the battle is over.

SECOND FEMALE: Hell, if there isn't, go to the bank and get more. Repay by installments from generation to generation. It's cool man! That's the way they used to do it many years ago. They used to say, "It's cool man!"

LEADER: O.K. Stop! We must fight the battle the prescribed way. When my hands are raised things are in our favor. When they're down, it'll go the other way. (*He makes a gesture to demonstrate.*)

> (*Two actors appear from the
> opposite sides of the stage. One
> carries a blue sign, the other a
> black sign.*)

LEADER: (*turns to the one with the blue sign*) You're creating a disturbance...... You may have heard the voice.. you may have thought He meant you... The Gospel is Greek... even the Alpha is not the Aleph; listen very close.... It's not the same sound, not even the same symbol. (*The other actor points gleefully to his sign and to himself. The leader turns to him with a short laugh*). He didn't mean you either... you can't impersonate what's hidden in the stars... (*points*). He's Aleph and he's a lie... You're the Yod and you too are the lie... lets not argue this one out. We decided to lie... we all lied... It seemed the right thing to do. It really still is and the time is not yet. As long as the "I" (*sound eeeeh*) is hidden in the stars. I am at war.. So let me raise my hands, I'm trying to show you... like this.

SOMEBODY: (*rolls in an inner-tube from a tire, the bigger the better.*) Come on- cut the symbolic stuff. Do you know what this stands for? This is an inner tube I took out of a tubeless tire. They put it in there, in the garage... to be extra safe... and now the tire blew and the inner-tube is leaking... anybody here has water?

ONE ACTOR: Tires are tested up the mountain. You'll see the signs, just make sure it's the right one, there are so many you may get confused.

> (*SOMEBODY runs off is called back*)

FIRST FEMALE: Wait. Today everything is closed for Memorial Day. Except the skywriters. I saw'em early this morning: Olé- sin no more up there with a big exclamation mark.. oh- and the supermarkets are open.

SECOND FEMALE: Let's get on with the war- Too much talk not enough action.

> (*They're already bringing in the wounded*)

ONE ACTOR: What's with him? Where's the blood?

THIRD ACTOR: Hodgkin's disease. Terminal. Two months at the utmost… I mean at the most. Stand away.. don't touch. It's not catching.. but you know, never know, death vibration.

ONE ACTOR: You can't make war if you don't know the rules, like being run over by a car.. that's not in the rules.. or like this here stretcher-case… if he doesn't know the rules let him stay out.. who needs him… he embarrasses our side… better lose the war than end up with a case like that.

SECOND ACTOR: Olé!

FIRST FEMALE: (*laughs*) Yeah, and sin no more!

ACT II

(The Leader is by himself... his voice is low, but directed at the audience).

LEADER: Both sides are afraid… it's not like before and the battle has not yet erupted. We've changed the order of the sounds.. outside they are still looking for matches to light the fuse. They don't know we changed the order… I-A-O-U-E (*repeats these sounds phonetically with increasing speed until the word YAHWEH emerges clearly*) ….They don't know we changed the order…. They don't know we changed the order…. Now it's A-I-E-O-U (*this is said very slowly*). I will change the order. No more sacrifices… no more battle lines across my way; across my Waaa(y), across my way, across my Waa (*laughingly repeats this like a chant*).

ONE ACTOR & ANOTHER ACTOR: (*entering*) What are you doing here? They're looking for you. The First Female just finished stitching the flag….we're ready… built a throne for you… eight legs. Built by Bezalel… that's what it says on the back. A good mark, four millennia of experience… building thrones.

LEADER: (*looks at them absently*) It's so hard to speak and to speak differently is frightening… only the dying understand……… and not many of those… when we finally can say it, everybody'll understand: the living and the dying. (*he points to the East*) That's East? That's where the sun comes up.

ANOTHER ACTOR: All those guys tell us the same thing (*turns to second female who just entered*). I'm tired of hearing the same thing. I need something <u>new</u>! What guarantee have we got that we'll win the battle with <u>him</u>? Suppose the others have one, too?

SECOND FEMALE: What's with you suddenly? A moment ago you were handing a throne over to him... and now you want something new. You don't trust, man...

ANOTHER ACTOR: I trusted alright.... That was before he started talking about the living and the dying... and the sun rising to the east. They decided that long before I went to school... it's not <u>me</u>, I say, what's suddenly with <u>him</u>? I had hopes he had something up his sleeve... some more re-incarnation information... something like <u>that</u>... that always makes me feel good.... If I get it in battle, at least I've something to look forward to. Maybe I'll be an Egyptian prince or princess next time.

LEADER: Who'll recognize me, when they can't get to the sound? For them I'm a broken record and they leave a throne for me.... a throne and eight legs... (*there is a commotion off stage*). Ah, they can't wait to start the battle and too scared to fire the first shot and they build a throne without a king. We need king-builders. Ha! Even if we had them, we'd only know how to construct one model: A built-in success/failure system, operating on high power... low power.

SECOND FEMALE: Look there are three separate incidents needed for the news-media.... we're going to be on all three networks, they'll show on all three.... the leader directing the war.... We'll show the throne first empty... that'll be the first shot... I think all three incidents must start out like that... the public won't understand the significance of all this, unless we do it this way. Then the leader comes in from the right of the frame... scan back to empty throne... show the preparations of our side for the battle... maybe a neutral can get us some shots of preparations from the other side.... Oh I forgot, this time there are no neutrals... we must do the best we can. And then the incidents... three separate confrontations... maybe two with our eyes closed and the last one with the eyes open... on the last one, close-ups of the faces of the dying. Maybe this is the best way to teach them.

LEADER: (*smiling*) Whom are you planning to teach? What are you planning to teach?
Teach Idiocy! We already live that…. Teach Compassion! After the Fact… too late.
Teach Anger! They are already afraid. Being afraid is what the world is all about.
Teach Futility! That's what the blind man feels when he stands in the field on a
moonless night… We're all blind. Whom are you planning to teach what? What do you
know that they don't know? Another principle? A new theory? It's not like that! You
may not even find it written on the dying faces… it's the living who do the interpreting.
You don't recognize your teacher! It's the greedy who's permitted to accumulate… to
prove to him that his possessions are futile. It's the poor who is permitted to survive in
his squalor to prove to him that his squalor is futile.   It's the hermit who is permitted to
shut himself in, to prove to him that his cave is futile. You don't recognize your teacher
and you will teach?

FIRST FEMALE: Haaaah, and who'll teach you to build the ship with which to cross the
great water? We must get there one way or another.

LEADER: The teacher of all teachers will let me build it and well….. so I may move on
to make room for the younger ones … before I do this I'm obliged to live my life. This
will help a little in building their ships… that's my hope at least… you see, I do still
hope. But I must move on, there's still too much ahead of me which the teacher needs to
tell me about before my walk is done. Let me go! Leave the throne empty, if its only use
is to arbitrate and regulate ambitions…. Yet even now I'm not sure. Of what use are its
eight legs, if it is to remain empty…. Even now I'm not sure.

FIRST FEMALE: You are afraid… by God, you're afraid… that's the last thing I would
have thought… I can see it inside of you, it's crawling around… if I can see it, others
will… it's crawling out of the corner of your eyes… you're scared… how can you
regulate the battle when you're not sure..?

LEADER: There's something I lost… something we all lose when we enter here. To
know is to know and miss it… I've lost neutrality… the missing item… absolute
neutrality. As long as I stand outside of that, I lose my rights, I am the thief and I have to
recover what I stole. Listen to the sounds….. Eeeee!…. somewhere in there lies the clue,
somewhere in there is Eeeden, sooner or later (*turns to face the First Female directly*)…
I shall find the way back to the place… to the wall of fear. You can't climb it because
the ladder is on the other side… and it's not like at Jericho… it won't be done with
trumpets…… The sound has to come from here (*points to an area below his navel*).
There's the entrance and the exit… and the exercise!!

FIRST FEMALE: (starts to rock back and forth in a dance figure) That's the exercise!

(Others appear out of
the wings in similar
dance motion)

That's the exercise! That's the exercise!

ACT III

The battle is here now, the heavy guns, the machine
guns…. Sporadic bursts…. And the wounded are brought
in and deposited among the audience…. There are no
visible wounds and there's no audible pain… the faces
are contorted and they sit or lie so still, they seem
already dead. ONE ACTOR enters, squats on the
ground, stares at a space in the audience but focuses at a
place closer in front of himself.

ONE ACTOR: If you could only see it out there… but then, you can't see in the dark…
it's too hard to see when it's inside of ourselves like that. If it weren't for the pain and
the wounded you couldn't even be sure it's really there… and that throne they placed him
in, sitting there on it's eight legs… If you were only able to see him sitting there in broad
daylight, inside that piece of furniture and its bench-mark, Bezalel. He just sat there.
Finally he turned to me… to me! Can you imagine the honor for me? He said, "I'm not
fit for the job." Then he got up and walked away… left the throne empty like that…
what was I supposed to do? Somebody had to do something… I couldn't leave it like
that. Empty. So I walked up there and sat down in there… then you should have been
there… all hell broke loose. They all wanted to sit there …. Yeah…. (*points to the*
audience). I bet you'd like to have sat in there yourselves… just didn't get the chance…
MEMBER OF THE AUDIENCE: What did the paper say today in your daily horoscope?
Mine said lie low… That's all I remember. So don't accuse me!

ONE ACTOR: (*opens his mouth as if to say something, changes his mind and slumps back into himself.*)

ANOTHER ACTOR: Why did you let them throw you off? The ass-hole who is sitting there now has straw for brains. Have you got any idea how many men we lost? It's incredible, nobody will survive... there are too many weapons and there's too much ammunition on both sides... we're tearing ourselves apart.

ONE ACTOR: (*despondent*) Nobody's fit to sit there, on that piece of furniture... eight legs but it can't walk, and no one can make it walk in the dark... benchmark, Bezalel... If we only knew how to stop the battle... it's a vicious circle... we can't make it walk while we're busy shooting and we can't see until we can make it walk and we can't stop shooting until we can see, and it's so dark inside I don't dare stop shooting, 'cause the others may have the last shot.

SECOND FEMALE: (*enters in a nurse's uniform*) Repeat! Repeat! That was very philosophical.....

A VOICE: Aaaaaaaiiiiii!

SECOND FEMALE: Hey, I like what you said about the last shot.

A VOICE: Ye! (*sound: "yay"*)

ONE ACTOR: Bring the war to a close! I can hear it when my mouth speaks.... Bring the War to a close!

SECOND FEMALE: Whom are you asking?

A VOICE: Ye he! (*sound: "yay-hay"*)

SECOND FEMALE: Who's on the Public Address System?

ONE ACTOR: Who's on the throne?

A VOICE: Aaaiiii!

ONE ACTOR: (*recognizes himself*) Bring the war to a close. (*Continues with awe in his voice*) I bring the war to a close. I look at my hands, my feet, I kick, I bring it all to me, every itch and scratch, my darkness, my love... I bring the war to a close with eight strokes of my pen. I change the order of my five worlds. I bring the war to a close... in A, in I, in E, in O, in U. In A.... I.... E.... O.... U.... (*his voice slurs*) A—I—E—O—U—A (*pauses here*) I—E—O—U—A; Jehovah... I-E-O-U-A-I bring the war to a close and a new sun...

> The others, one by one, slowly at first,
> hesitantly, then with steadily increasing
> volume join as one voice:

A—I—E—O—U—A—I—E—O—U—A—I bring the war to a close
....I bring the war to a close...

EPILOGUE

(None are left now except one of them and his audience; he's the one who replaced the author. He now reads from a paper):

It's all over… the author got tired of writing. You may remember they chose me for his stand-in. That too is over. And it's written here that this is a good time for my own comments, so…. (*ad lib*).

Carl was always working, no matter what the media, or how his health changed, illness eventually took over control of his body and memory. He said, "I've accepted it but I don't like it. The access to my memory is becoming more difficult. That's a problem."

He avidly kept expanding his perspective. Observant, absorbing everything, he kept a journal in which his trembling hands wrote his poetry. "Poetry is concrete. You can hold it in your hand." His drawings are very detailed and abstract, he wrote, "Whatever comes out, it's spontaneous. They express the visions in my mind."

"I went through a period of desperation. I had to find myself." He said, "What led me to search is that I had to find rationale for what happened to me during the war and I couldn't find it in most religions."

Carl's dreams were put into turmoil when Adolf Hitler came into power and he was forced to flee Germany. His parents put him on a transport to the US at age 13, "I was known as an enemy alien." He said. He was adopted by the Flarshiem family where they lived in Cincinnati, Ohio. Carl never saw his parents again but his brother, Alfred, survived and eventually made it to the US.

When Carl moved to Santa Fe in 1971, he took a new name, Hi Ka Lu, a spiritual name he took from Japanese philosophy. "I could basically find out who I was without having to listen to someone else tell me. The principals of faith seemed to answer questions that I had about my life."

"Play for Puppets" which he also drew the illustrations, is filled with axioms, pointed comments about the state of the world, it is humorous, but sometimes very serious. It could be said that the play has sound-bytes that seem to have roots in existentialism. But the principals of the sounds and the order of perception described in the Second and Third Civilizations can clearly be observed in the characters he brought to life in the play.

There is evidence of cruelty, when the characters who are deep in the concrete perception of the Second Civilization, characterize war, anger and intuition that is colored by a generational gender inequality. Towards the end, the audience observes changes take place on concepts of the cosmos. Ideas of the race for equality, that became just another competitive grip for control, give way to a new order. Our attention is focused in new ways of interaction.. (New Mexican, article A 12, Monday, December 21, 1987 Santa Fe NM).

In addressing the concept of the theatre, a beginning, and ideas develop as an expression or if you will, an exhale of breath by the artist or author. The exhale then exists, however briefly, into the world. The artist attempts to reach out into the world and would like to be understood by all as "this is the exhale of my breath." The breath becomes the world at the time of its term, included in the mix are fashion, trends, interests, political area and the like that involve the human integration of the cosmos and understanding of what that looks like.

I would suppose that the cosmos could be thought of as a theater of light and darkness and forces. Our community is like a group or a set with people who are groping for meaning in their life. The isolation is like pain that somehow must be willed away.

From its very beginning, theatre is one way to stop the pain because we can see in front of ourselves those things we try to hide or close our eyes to. Our thoughts, in trying to make sense of our experiences, are one long stream of self-talk like a snake with a mental pair of scissors. Our memory continually stores our experiences in dreams and substance that we try to put away. Like an apothecary chest of herbs and smells, the memories triggered by the smells bring to mind thoughts either pleasant or not.

A Play for Puppets drops the reader, viewer, experiencer or whatever, into an allegory that is very similar to what Carl began with his journey as a poet of concrete poetry (page 10 of this book) and the defending of the manifesto that both began as a definition that one could digest intellectually and the moving target of the art movement as it grew and changed over the years.

Artists continually wrestle with the esthetic nature of line and the word, in reality, the spirit in the letter, itself. Carl brings to life a world with certainty that is something like what we live in but the description is both found in the night of our consciousness and the intention of the heart. It demands our attention, we are being asked to take responsibility and the viewer is not only taught, led, and directed, but in turn becomes the director.

The awareness brings together a certain holding of the breath as Carl's voice is tasted in the ideas presented about life as it disappears into dream.

Each year our understanding grows and different concepts are tried out and either kept or discarded in our community soup called knowledge. Something like this might be viewed as energy ebbing and flowing around "rocks" and "mud" and other obstacles as it meanders down the grade of a hillside.

Structure also has a certain universality, in that it is understood as a force that contains, or maintains the energy, much like a river bank is a division of water and earth. Color and other manifestations then in turn take the form of the phenomenon moving through the river, a manifestation of change and intention. This is something of a universal painting that not only is a constant of frequency and duration but demands attention in the merits of capturing our interest and curiosity.

The problem is in capturing this universal view and describing it to others. There must be rules developed, understanding of how a proper diagram must be drawn up and symbols of language and agreed upon meaning. By the time all this process is assembled the universality of the phenomenon being described is no longer universal. Art imitates, man, nature, color, form, etc. what does the concept of God imitate? We then become disciples of describing that. Carl askes the question: Does Art Imitate God? If so, what does that look like?

Theatre involves, a reflection of everything in the cosmos, political, and trend. It is a canvas of the universal and like breath, is created, expressed and then changed into something else, ultimately to disappear into time. The moment art, visually, is expressed into a concrete substance it has a decided modality and interpretation. In looking at Carl's work there is a form, structure, movement and change. The universality of it is that the images caught in the structure are like a snapshot, so universal, it could be said that anyone looking at it would likely see the same image, shape and form without descending into the development of rules to interpret what is being seen.

However, as I am placed into the position of critique and "director," I too have a description of how to look at this canvas of sound and movement. In appreciation of the work I find it helpful to look at the white first, Carl describes the white as a void, the void is our interpretation of order, and it is the first phenomenon that we as the observer encounter. Then the manifestation of sound, the accompanying movement and color becomes the new structure of substance and the form. From that we can then describe the feeling, the mode and finality.

The last order is in describing our feeling from reaction of the phenomenon that we as travelers observe. Are we involved in the reaction as the artist breathes out the creation? Are we as much a part of the creating as what is being created? In the "Play for Puppets," that question has been answered. In the play the chair with the many legs becomes the vehicle, form, and physical conveyance such as the canvas of the work becomes the physical conveyance to our senses. Is some part of who we are, driving the conveyance?

So, this is a *"good time for your own comments···"*

ABOUT THE AUTHOR

Dave F. Farbrook lived most of his life in New Mexico, with over 25 years professional experience in research, has compiled a rich preface of his father's accomplishments and conclusions. Carl Fernbach-Flarsheim wrote his essays, plays and lectures under his Sage Name, HiKaLu, after 1971 when he moved to New Mexico. This Play was one of the sub-books in The Boolean Theatre, a book written by Dave F. Farbrook on the history of his father as a contemporary artist and poet between 1962 through 1985.

Mr. Farbrook has authored essays, a cookbook, a blogsite, and as of this publication, broadcasts with Albuquerque NOW! Podcast.   Additionally, he has edited 4 children's empowerment books with JJ Alexander. He has assisted with grant writing for several non-profit organizations in urban improvement and STEM/MSAP education. He has been blessed with a daughter and a son, both who are very successful in their areas of interest.

www.ingramcontent.com/pod-product-compliance
Lightning Source LLC
LaVergne TN
LVHW061229060426
835509LV00012B/1480

* 9 7 8 1 7 3 7 8 0 7 6 0 5 *